A Call from Nan

By Sally Cowan

“Let’s go to see Nan!”
said Dad.

“We are all set!” I said.

“The van is full!” said Mum.
“Can Pip the bulldog fit?”

Pip is small.
She can sit with me.

We had a picnic.

Pip's ball fell into a fox den!

Next, Pip rolled in some mud.

I had to pull her out!

Mum got us all a bun from a stall.

Dad and I sat on a wall in the sun.

Then Dad got a call from Nan.

So, we went for a swim.

We got the mud off Pip.

And we all had a ball!

CHECKING FOR MEANING

1. Who was the family going to visit? *(Literal)*
2. Why couldn't they visit Nan? *(Literal)*
3. Did Pip enjoy rolling in the mud? How do you know? *(Inferential)*

EXTENDING VOCABULARY

rolled	What is the base of the word *rolled*? What does the word *rolled* mean in *Pip rolled in some mud*? What else can *roll* mean?
pull	What are some things that you can pull? What makes something difficult to pull? What word means the opposite of *pull*?
ball	On the last page of the story, what does the word *ball* mean?

MOVING BEYOND THE TEXT

1. Who is your favourite friend or relative to visit?
2. What are some other ways to travel besides driving in a car?
3. Have you ever travelled with a pet? Why might it be difficult to travel with pets?
4. What can you do to make the time pass during long trips?

SPEED SOUNDS

oll	ull	all

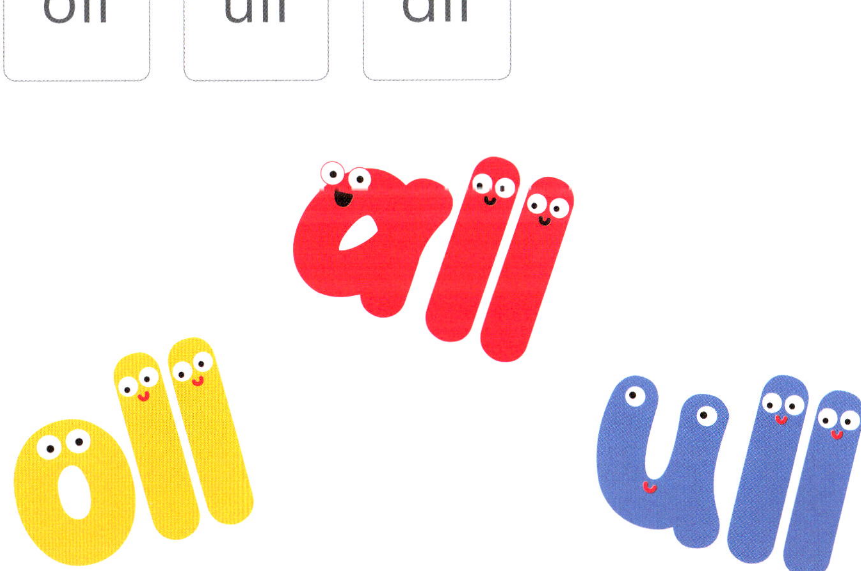

PRACTICE WORDS

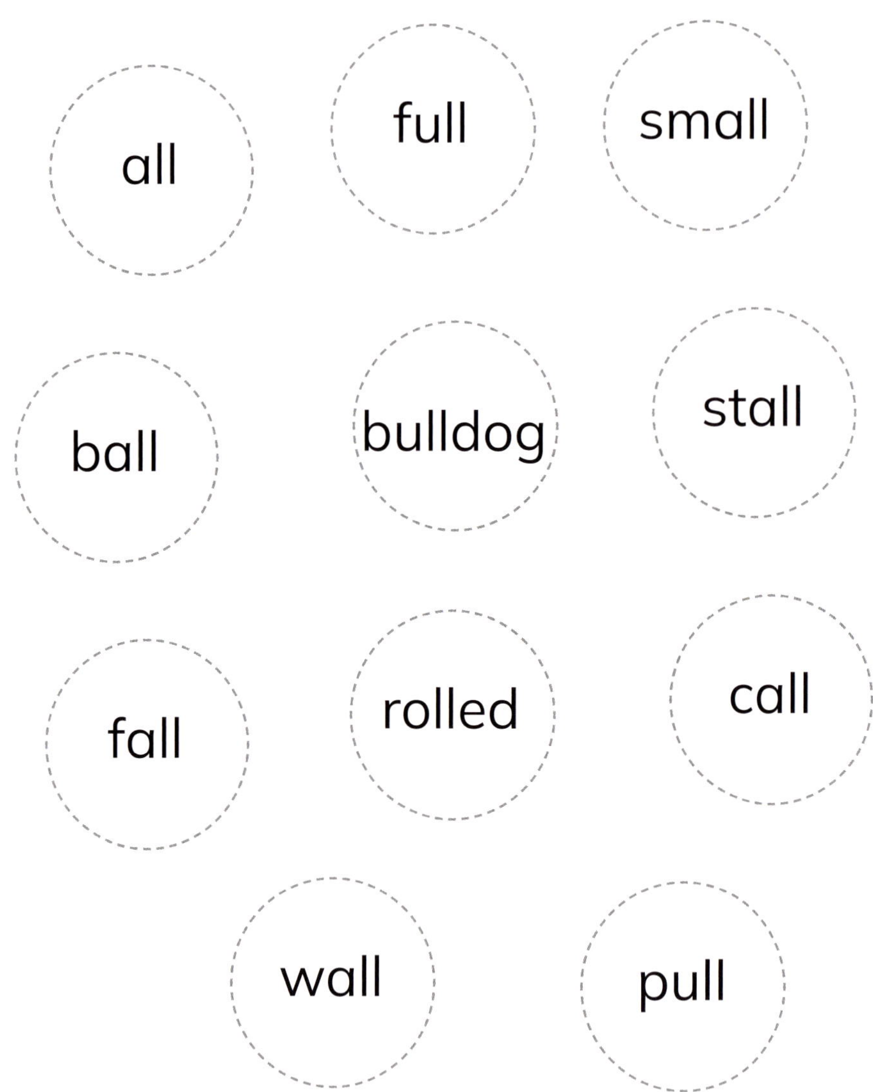